Conte

Tune: Ministres de l'Éternel 77.77.77 EH 258

In the springtime of my life,
  In the freshness of my youth,
Then you called to me in love,
  Led me in the path of truth;
There to you I gave my soul,
  And you cleansed and made me whole.

In the summer of my life,
  Now you guide me and defend;
On your loveliness I gaze,
  On your providence depend;
In this summertime of love,
  All your faithfulness I prove.

When the autumn of my life
  Comes, with evening fruitfulness,
Shield me as the shadows grow
  From encroaching weariness;
May the evening of my days
  Thus be filled with prayer and praise.

When the winter of my life
  Threatens me with pain and death,
Leave me not in loneliness
  To its cold and icy breath;
Breathe upon me from above
  And enfold me in your love.

God of nature's moving force,
  Lord of season's changing days,
All creation gives you thanks,
  And redemption shouts your praise;
Let my days be filled with grace
  Till I gaze upon your face.

SSF (R)

Life's Changing Seasons

☐ CHRISTIAN SPIRITUALITY SERIES ☐

Remember Me
Praying the Jesus Prayer
Praying the Bible

Life's Changing Seasons

Christian Growth and Maturity

Brother Ramon SSF

Marshall Pickering

Marshall Morgan and Scott
Marshall Pickering
3 Beggarwood Lane, Basingstoke, Hants RG23 7LP, UK

First published in 1988 by Marshall Morgan and Scott Publications Ltd
Part of the Marshall Pickering Holdings Group
A subsidiary of the Zondervan Corporation

British Library CIP Data

Ramon, *Brother*
Life's changing seasons.—(Evangelical spirituality series).
1. Christian life—1960 –
I. Title II. Series
248.4 BV4501.2

ISBN: 0-551-01543-8

Text set in 10/11pt Baskerville by Brian Robinson Ltd. Buckingham

Printed in Great Britain by Henry Ling Ltd., at the Dorset Press, Dorchester, Dorset.

Introduction: Nature's Changing Seasons

> 'While the earth remains, seedtime and harvest, cold and heat, summer and winter, day and night, shall not cease.' (Genesis 8:22)

I have just returned from our monastery vegetable garden. August gives way to September, and fruitfulness and abundance calls out from every plant and tree. There are carrots, beans, marrows and cucumbers; there are onions, lettuces, purple sprouting brassica, spinach and celery. The greenhouse bears tomatoes, peppers and aubergines, and the orchard trees carry damsons, cherries, quince, apples and pears. Within the garth there are figs, plums and sweet apples and the bees have delivered up their load of honey, filled with the sweetness of clover and all the flowers of summer.

Some of our professed brothers and novices come from evangelistic and social labour in urban and inner city areas with all their turmoil, grime and stress, and find in this place not only a house of prayer, where the adoration of God and daily eucharist is offered in faith and love, but also a house of fruitfulness, beauty and rest. Refreshment and renewal is found here, and a peace that bears witness to the reconciling nature of the Gospel.

Don't get me wrong – I am not advocating a sentimental nature-mysticism divorced from the reality of pain or the need for compassion, versified in these Victorian lines:

The kiss of the sun for pardon,
The song of the rain for mirth,
One is nearer God's heart in a garden
Than anywhere else on earth.

No! It depends what goes on in the garden, for Eden can be glory – or estrangement. There are many examples of broken lives, stress, anxiety and downright sinfulness exposed here, to the searching light of God's love and truth. Repentance and restitution are as much part of our lives as thanksgiving and adoration. Some of our houses are based in the inner city, and the loving, forgiving presence of God is found there too. After all, that is what the Incarnation is all about. Nevertheless, this is a wonderful place to experience the changing of the seasons, the glory of the night sky, the rising and setting of the sun, and the mists and rain that speak of fruitfulness and peace.

In this book I want to share with you what I call 'the changing seasons of life'. I mean that we are not static beings with a fixed human nature, caught and trapped in programmed lives in which there is no process of change, vitality, elasticity. Change and flux is of the essence of life. You can never step into the same river twice, for it is forever flowing, moving, changing. I am not now speaking of the rapid technological change and political ideological upheavals that are the cause of much of our twentieth century apprehension and stress. Neither am I speaking of the bloody revolutionary changes which many look for. These changes often mean that political hopes of a violent and sanguinary nature only replace one set of power-hungry leaders by another, initiating another period of totalitarian oppression in which the poor are made poorer and the rich rake in the gains. We must work for positive, non-violent political change, and be able to move, adapt and be versatile in our world. But we can only do this as we participate in the process of the changing seasons. The sowing and reaping, the planting, flowering, budding and fruiting of creation is rooted in the faithfulness and immutability of God:

> We blossom and flourish like leaves on the tree;
> We wither and perish; but nought changes Thee.

This means that within the unity and immutability of the Godhead there is not only basic triunity, but a rich diversity and flow of loving compassion that allows creation to live and breathe within the fulness of God. The pulse of the world is the heartbeat of God, and the dynamic presence of the living God is immanent in his creation. In him we live, move and have our being; from him we come and to him we go. Creation is the dance, the rhythm, the harmony of God, and earth, sea and sky are caught up in the revelation of his love.

Nature's changing seasons reflect the diverse aspects of our physical, mental and spiritual lives, and to be able to identify with, and experience these changes within our own psyche, is to open ourselves to the process of transformation which is the work of the Holy Spirit within us. The Holy Spirit is the wind of God that blows in creation, and the breath of God that breathes within the human soul. It is mysterious and life-giving, and the powers of the new birth are closely linked to the intimate and dynamic breathing of God within creation and within the believer.

This means that there is a place and a time for laughter and tears, for rejoicing and melancholy, for the oil of gladness and the ashes of mourning. It means that proclamation and contemplation are two aspects of a full-orbed Christian life, and that the dark night of the soul can be more productive than singing in the Spirit.

I was perplexed as a young Christian due to lack of teaching. There were times when I could laugh and sing in praise and adoration of God for the beauty of creation and the joy of redemption. That was acceptable, for was not joy one of the marks of salvation, and was not this the face that the newly-converted presented to the world? But I could not deny that there were times of pain and tears, and I don't only mean the bearing of another's sorrows in intercession or compassion, but a sharing of the misery, mortality and finitude of the human condition. There was the loss of sensual joy, the experience of feeling the privation of belonging to a race and a people which knew mortality, finitude and sorrow. There was also the sense of the heave and swell of the sea and its thudding reverberations through the ocean caves echoing and re-echoing the world's sorrow in the absence of God, or revealing something of what has been called the dark face of God.

All these things and many more are part of the wholeness of christian experience, and maturity means a deliverance from the infancy and adolescence of continual mountain-top alleluias. The higher you ascend the mountain, the more the mysterious mists will swirl around your head and heart, until you can only be led by the providential mercy of God and by the interior light within.

This little book is one of encouragement and enlightenment, for if the believer realises the changing of his spiritual seasons, the need to be open, pliable, versatile and sensitive to the Holy Spirit, then the whole of life will be taken up into the whole of God's creative-redemptive cycle. Then sunshine and rain, summer and winter, seedtime and harvest will *all* be part of the ongoing life of God within the soul, and the vistas of eternity will open up within. The path into the deep and hidden mystery of God will lead to a more profound understanding of yourself, your neighbour, of our common humanity, and of God himself.

Brother Ramon SSF
The Society of St Francis
Season of Autumn 1987

Spring

Arise, my love, my fair one,
and come away;
for lo, the winter is past . . .
The flowers appear on the earth,
the time of singing has come,
and the voice of the turtledove
is heard in our land.
(Song of Solomon 2:11f)

The Spring of In

There is something beau
or animal full of the risin
skipping with sheer exuberance
And in the heart there is hope and
joyful expectancy. To be young, w
heaven, when there is an immediacy
overflow of vital energy that communicate
sheer joy. Wordsworth catches the mood:

> Bliss was it in that dawn to be alive,
> But to be young was very heaven.

To be able to retain such a feeling, to remain buoyant with the hope, the joy, the excitement of being alive, is a great gift. Not only do I *remember* the way I used to run along the sands, roll in the waves, sing and shout in the wind – but I still do it. That is part of the joy of my solitude. But when others are around I am more circumspect! I've just realised in writing that word that it literally means 'looking around'. Perhaps that's the trouble – I can afford to be a child when I am alone, but am careful of my image when in company. Too much of such circumspect behaviour can lead to a loss of vital life and joy, a sedate sterility that is socially acceptable, but which imprisons me in a respectable society of well-behaved adults. This also Wordsworth understood when he wrote:

> Heaven lies about us in our infancy!
> Shades of the prison-house begin to close
> Upon the growing boy.

I must retain my childlike wonder and abandon – my spring-time. I must not become childish but allow the river of joy to flow through my being, bringing life and fertility wherever it flows. The immediacy of infancy and the energy and curiosity my heart, enthusing others with

The Spring of the Incarnation

Springtime is the period of new life. The angel Gabriel appears to Mary in the springtime of her physical life and of her spiritual experience. The wonder of new life is communicated to her, and she trembles with apprehension and joy. Gabriel's words are like a spring torrent:

> The Holy Spirit will come upon you,
> and the power of the Most High will overshadow you;
> therefore the child to be born will be called holy,
> the Son of God.

Here is Jesse's tree that budded, here the sap of the new creation rises, here the mortal woman becomes pregnant with the immortal seed, and Mary's womb becomes the dwelling-place of God. Mary is the virgin who is pregnant with divinity, and the new springtime has begun. Mary has been wooed by the divine Love, and how beautifully mysterious it is for her as she feels the stirrings of new life within her body as spring gives way to summer in the first springtime of new life for the world.

Mary is the image of the Church and the prototype of the believer. All those who are wooed by the Holy Spirit, who hear the sighing of the Spirit in the bondage of creation, can open the womb of their hearts, and the powers of the new birth will become operative within the mystery of the generative powers of mystical life. To become pregnant with Christ, to bear within yourself the eternal Word, to know the indwelling of the Son of God – this is what it means to be born again, and to allow the process to continue within your individual life, and within the fellowship of the Church, which is the bride of Christ.

The Spring of Conversion

To turn from the cold and barren winter of sin, from the darkness and paralysis of a life in the icy grip of death, and to surrender to the sweet, warm and fragrant airs of forgiveness, acceptance, reconciliation and love, is the springtime of the soul. The creative powers of new life are at work, the sap is rising, the tight buds are opening, the air is balmy and inebriating, and the smell of creation is wild and ecstatic. Conversion is the bursting forth of new life, the stirring of the creative powers of love, and the soul cries out in gladness, because creation itself seems wholly new to the eyes of one who has gazed upon the crucified Jesus:

> For you shall go out in joy,
> and be led forth in peace:
> the mountains and the hills before you
> shall break forth into singing,
> and all the trees of the field
> shall clap their hands.

Man belongs to earth and heaven. His physical roots sink deep into the soil of mortality and finitude, and his spiritual roots into the soil of divinity and immortality. He is animal, and therefore the joy of his physicality, his sensuality, his sexuality in its innocence, is all part of the creative drama in which he shares with the animal creation the tremendous joy of simply being alive. But he is also endowed with divinity, for the eternal Word enlightens every man that comes into the world – God breathed into Adam the breath of life, and man became a living soul.

Adam's natural springtime should have given way to the glorious natural procession of the seasons, involving him in the cyclic movement of the divine immanence in the world. But the garden of Eden became overrun with thorns and briars. The roots of man's divinity became poisoned, twisted and choked with the brambles of sin, and paradise became a wilderness. In this sad story every man is Adam and every woman Eve, and in his alienation from the life of God Adam hides in the garden, afraid and ashamed, under condemnation and judgement, with the roots of bitterness and rebellion bearing fruit in suffering and sin. Paradise becomes Paradise lost, and Adam and Eve become wandering vagrants on the face of the earth, barred from the tree of life and bringing forth according to their kind in rebellion, murder and bloodshed.

Into this icy winter of sin shines the Sun of Righteousness, and the warmth of his rising dispels the darkness, radiates the earth with the flow of spring, gently melting the snow and ice, and releasing the life-giving waters of the earth. The cold hardness of the ground is softened to enable the new life to spring forth, and the rays of the sun draw out the colour, the fragrance and the beauty of plants and flowers. Springtime is upon us, vitality is within and around us, and we are all caught up in the cosmic movement of the divine life-force which is the breathing of the Holy Spirit over creation:

> When you send forth your Spirit they are created,
> and you renew the face of the earth.

Thomas Aquinas said: *Gratia non tollit naturam,* grace does not suppress nature. When we separate man's natural from his supernatural life we do so at our peril. It is one life, and the shining of the Sun of Righteousness with healing in his wings brings life to the body, soul and spirit of man. The regenerative powers of conversion restore to man his childlike wonder, his spiritual faculties and even his bodily awareness.

Of course, conversion, though it may be manifested in a moment, like St Paul's experience on the Damascus road, or Wesley's experience in the warming of his heart in Aldersgate Street, London, in 1738, nevertheless takes a lifetime to engage the whole of man's being. Salvation becomes sanctification, and conversion is the gradual turning of all our powers of body, mind and spirit to God. There are three tenses of salvation: I *have been* saved – I *am being* saved – I *shall be* saved. Salvation is of the whole person and the whole community, and is consummated ultimately in the vision of God, in union with God, in the life of the world to come. Grace regenerates, elevates, illuminates and fills nature with the very life of God, and the process carries us into and through death, into the new springtime of eternity.

The Spring of Love

Such an extension of the concept of conversion brings us to the mystical life. The call of the lover in the Song of Solomon is one which draws the beloved out of her cold winter of lovelessness into the springtide of love. The call of the lover is the mystical call to union with the beloved, and the true end of conversion, though it must needs traverse the way of purgation, leads to illumination and union in love. For union is ever the end of love, and such a consummation is the beginning of a new cycle of loving adoration in which lover and beloved are united in ever more intimate and mutual embraces of unitive love.

It is not enough to turn one's back upon the winter of sin, to know forgiveness and reconciliation with God. It is not enough to be justified, cleared of all that was against us and to rejoice in the assurance of sins forgiven. That is only the beginning. The springtime of conversion must go on. The process of the new birth has to do with the intimate mutuality of indwelling – Christ dwelling within the heart of the believer – the Holy Spirit dwelling within the temple of the Church. Jesus said that he is the vine and we are the branches; therefore the life-giving sap must rise and flow into all the branches of the vine until the flowers and fruits of love are manifested. We are the Body of Christ, and the divine life of the head must flow through all the members and the mystical life of God must bring into play all the creative faculties of the body. The Church is the Bride of Christ, and he is the heavenly Bridegroom. So the bride is wooed by the divine Love and surrenders herself continually and completely to the intimate life of union, so that they become one flesh, ultimately participating in the very life of God. What joy and energy, what hope and expectation then, in the springtime of love.

Meditation

1 FIND a quiet place and sit or kneel in a relaxed posture.
2 ALLOW all tension to drain away, and slow your breathing until it is deeper, without strain or stress.
3 AFFIRM God's loving presence and commit yourself to his care: 'In the Name of the Father † and of the Son, and of the Holy Spirit'.
4 READ the second chapter of the *Song of Solomon*, slowly and reflectively.
5 LISTEN to Vivaldi's 'Spring' from *The Four Seasons* (EMI: TC-EMX 2009) or other suitable music.
6 OPEN YOURSELF to the thoughts of the chapter, allowing the Lord to carry you where he will (allowing 15 to 30 minutes).
7 EMERGE gently from the meditation, offering thanks extemporaneously, or in the words: 'The grace of our Lord Jesus Christ, the love of God and the fellowship of the Holy Spirit be with us now and always. Amen.'
8 LIVE your life in the awareness and experience of the springtime of God in your heart.

Summer

From the fig tree learn its lesson: as soon as its branch becomes tender and puts forth its leaves, you know that summer is near.

(Mark 13:28)

Summer: Discernment and Activity

Jesus calls for a summer-time of discernment and activity. Look for the signs, be busy in application, apply mind and heart to an understanding of the times and seasons. While the secular world used to sing of 'those lazy, hazy, crazy days of summer', I remember associating those lovely hot summer days of my childhood (where have they gone?), with Bishop William How's hymn:

> Summer suns are glowing
> Over land and sea;
> Happy light is flowing,
> Bountiful and free.
> Everything rejoices
> In the mellow rays;
> All earth's thousand voices
> Swell the psalm of praise.

If springtime indicates the first flush of new love for Christ, then summer is the time of discernment, evaluation, the area of activity and loving service. Our creative faculties are put at the disposal of the Lord for whom love is confessed, so that love of God and neighbour come together in an ordered and disciplined life.

Summer can be both exhilarating and tiring, and certainly there is constant need of rest from the drought and heat of the noon-tide sun, and times of shadow-refreshment and quietness are indicated. When the disciples were busy in their preaching, teaching and healing work, Jesus would say: 'Come apart and rest awhile.' And when he was continually thronged by multitudes of people, he would not run himself into the ground with hyper-active exhaustion, but extricate himself from the crowds and go up the mountain, into the wilderness or to some place of quietness like the village of Bethany, for communion with his Father, renewing strength and vitality.

The summertime of service becomes a prison for some who chain themselves to the grinding mill of frenetic activity, believing themselves to be indispensable, or with an obsession of being acceptable to others, or afraid to stop lest their own interior emptiness and bankruptcy be exposed.

The summertime of life should be a time of increasing fruitfulness, of allowing the springtime sap to do its work so that the buds either flower or come to fruit effortlessly, according to the rhythm of the seasons. There is no push and strain in nature, for if one forces a bud to open, forces a butterfly from its chrysalis or a dragonfly from its capsule, then certain immaturity, injury or death follows. An active life that is continually under strain, and in which stress is the major factor of daily existence is one which will reveal frustration, impatience and counter-productive attitudes to others, and will itself end up in cardiac, gastric or hyper-tensive problems which will eventually lead to premature incapacity and death.

Because summertime brings heat and exhaustion care must be taken over sustenance and rest. Therefore, engagement on active service must be alternated with periods of retreat, reflection and recreation. One of the ways to do this is by taking a day a week in recreation and relaxation. It should incorporate rest, exercise, mental and physical stimulation, according to one's personal needs, with an oasis of contemplative prayer. If you have a sedentary job, then exercise such as walking, jogging, squash, cycling, swimming, etc. is called for. If you have a manual or heavy job, then your recreation need not be as physically demanding, and periods of reading, study and/or the learning of a language or an instrument may be what you need. Those who have the care of small children are most neglected in this area – if you are *not* such a person, why not baby-sit occasionally?

As to prayer, meditation and contemplative experience, you ought to think of joining a prayer group, learning a few aids or techiques of meditative prayer, and considering going on a retreat for an extended period. If you are unemployed, retired, or have no job for other reasons, then your life needs to be organised, for there is such a thing as *accidie*. *Accidie*, in some of its manifestations, is a kind of sloth, boredom, tedium, listlessness or paralysis that comes from inaction and induces torpitude of body and mind, and a deterioration of spiritual awareness. The old Desert Fathers used to call it 'the destruction that wastes at noonday' (Psalm 91:6), and it is certainly the affliction of high summer. The antidote is usually basic manual work such as getting your hands and feet into the soil, application of mind to a disciplined study and friendship and fellowship with other Christians, co-operating in service for others.

Summertime Heat

Then there is the kind of spiritual drought that comes about either from neglect or culpable sin. It was a hot day when David the king went up onto the roof-top, and there he 'happened' to see Bathsheba, Uriah's beautiful wife, bathing. He looked, he lingered, he lusted and he nursed and coddled his lust – and the obvious thing happened! The trouble is that this kind of noonday lust doesn't end there. It is frustrating in itself and usually reaches out to harm others. The sexual frustration that follows sheer animal lust without regard to the fragility and sacredness of human relationship often produces a backlash, and either sours that relationship or leads to deceit, coarseness or cruelty. To hide his sin and protect his reputation, Kind David ordered Uriah to be put into the front-line of battle, got him killed, and thought he would get away with it. This is the sin of the noontide heat, which dries up the dew of one's own soul and also sucks the other person dry. There followed a prophetic word of judgment, and David's repentance (the story is found in 2 Samuel chapters 11 and 12). It is a long haul back, involving a child's death, bereavement and much heartache, and in David's moving psalm of repentance, *miserere*, he cries out:

Your hand was heavy upon me day and night:
and my moisture was dried up like a drought in summer.

Sin unresolved, unrepented of, and unforgiven works ravaging destruction within the human psyche, and often has devastating effects upon relationships. Sin unresolved and repressed works an even greater evil in the soul, and emerges in subtler, negative and fouling manifestations, working evil abroad, until the root of the matter is exposed, examined, confessed, forsaken and forgiven. The sure way to dry up the moisture of the soul is to allow love and compassion to leak away in sin and pride. The result is a shrivelled and wizened fruit that lacks moisture, juice and sweetness. How many shrivelled souls there are who have dried up in the summer-heat of cynicism, pride and hardness of heart. Summertime should be a period of loving sevice, when all the springtime sap brings forth the fruit of compassion and the flowers and foliage of abundance and full growth. The preaching, teaching and healing ministry of Jesus was the summertime of his service. It was a time of being anointed by the Holy Spirit for the healing of the sick and the restoration of the lost and alienated. It was a time for the destruction of dark powers, not a time for summer-heat to dry up the juices of the soul, resulting in the leaking away of life-giving sap into uselessness and frustration.

Integration of Faculties

Summertime is also the beginning of the integration of adult faculties. There is an enthusiasm, zest and idealism in the springtime of youth that tends to hasty conclusions. The bible speaks of a zeal without knowledge, a judgment without mature reflection. Youth's enthusiasm, because it is enthusiasm, tends to make snap judgments of a black/white variety. It is easier to categorise than to evaluate with wisdom, and those who don't agree with me are apt to be put into category-boxes that determine who and what they are, and where they are going.

If I think I am 'saved' and he doesn't agree with me, then he must be 'lost'; I am a sheep and he is a goat; I am on the narrow road to life and he is on the broad road to destruction; I am a child of God and he is a child of the devil. This idealistic judgmental attitude of youth operates on political, religious and cultural levels, but if it persists into later life and experience, it is a sign of arrested adolescence, of lack of maturity. Simple, human, day-to-day existence is often found in shades of grey, and compassion comes from closeness to the needs of people. Growth in compassion is a sure sign of maturity, and a drought of the dew of heaven is sometimes seen in the shrivelled hypocrisy of bigoted belief. The sad thing is that there are sects, groupings within the churches, and exclusivist societies which encourage bigotry and dogmatism in their concern for 'pure' doctrine, enslaving their adherents in years of religious and political bondage, which is the antithesis of the liberating, loving and compassionate Gospel of Jesus.

The practice of meditation leads a person to examine himself in depth and honesty, exposing his whole self to the divine Love. It then becomes clear that there are all the possiblities for evil and pride within himself, as well as the potential for wisdom and holiness. Sometimes it is better to stumble and fall rather than live seemingly faultlessly, if the result is a chastened, disciplined, forgiven and compassionate spirit. Here lies the pathway from springtime to summer, the psychic journey from child to adult, the difficult path from zeal to wisdom, without a loss of infectious and joyful enthusiasm.

Meditation

1 – 3 As in the *Meditation* section for Spring

4 READ one of the stories of Jesus'healing compassion (eg The healing of the leper in Mark 1:35-45)

5 LISTEN to Vivaldi's 'Summer' from *The Four Seasons*, or other suitable music

6 – 8 As in the *Meditation section for Spring*

Autumn

They came to Bethlehem at the beginning of the barley harvest.

(Ruth 1:22)

Harvest and Fruitfulness

Carl Gustav Jung charts the course of psychological and emotional maturity by a process he calls *Individuation*, and late summer to autumn is the appropriate seasonal image. This is a process involving time, patience, evaluation and integration. It is a natural pilgrimage and everyone is called upon to constant self-knowledge, adjustment and a wisdom that embraces and uses one's natural creative faculties, while realising one's limitations. The way forward is the way of integration, bringing all one's powers together into a personal wholeness in which all aspects of one's character are examined, accepted and cherished. There may be a call to change and transformation involved, but no call to repression or regression, and no hiding from any aspect that is revealed, but rather a facing up to it, and a positive sharing, leading to mutual understanding and gradual transformation.

All this has its spiritual counterpart. The work of salvation is not simply a 'moment' but a process, though it may have a definite starting-point of emotional or intellectual crisis and decision. The process of sanctification means the transformation, by the indwelling power of the Holy Spirit, of one's life, until the radiance and beauty of the risen Jesus shines from the believer. It affirms that all of life's circumstances are taken up into the creative will of God, so that all things may work together for good.

When Naomi returned to Bethlehem after many years of suffering bereavement and loneliness in the land of Moab, she was in the autumn of her life, but she was returning to her beginnings, coming back to *Beth-lechem*, the house of bread, and it was the beginning of the barley-harvest. There are new beginnings in the autumn, and it is wonderful to meet older Christians who have a lovely childlike spirit of wonder and enthusiasm, who have not allowed the drought of summer to evaporate or drain away their joy and enthusiasm. John Keats wrote his autumn ode on a purely natural and seasonal level, but its nostalgic beauty calls for a profound spiritual application of his lines:

> Season of mists and mellow fruitfulness!
> Close bosom-friend of the maturing sun;
> Conspiring with him how to load and bless
> With fruit the vines that round the thatch-eaves run;
> To bend with apples the moss'd cottage-trees,
> And fill all fruit with ripeness to the core;
> To swell the gourd, and plump the hazel shells
> With a sweet kernel; to set budding more,
> And still more, later flowers for the bees,
> Until they think warm days will never cease,
> For Summer has o'er-brimmed their clammy cells.

Harvest time in scripture is an occasion for offering to God and thoughtful care of the neighbour (Lev. 23:10,11,22; Deut 24:19), and though diligent hard work and weeping accompanied the sowing, reaping took place in joy, thanksgiving and fruitfulness (Psalm 126:6).

Suffering and Mortality

There is, in autumn, the mellow wisdom and tranquillity that comes with maturity. But there is also the realisation of mortality, with many reminders of suffering and sickness serving as tokens of the weakness and fragility of our mortal lives.

It is easy to carry the enthusiasm and joy of youth when the blood is coursing in your veins, when breathlessness comes only from hard exercise or excitement and when the wind rushes through your hair as you run or ride with speed. Tumbling over in the waves or rolling down a turfed hillside, you cannot help but shout with joy, dance with vitality and sing with effervescence. But when breathlessness comes with *little* exertion, the night is spent fretfully because of the constant nagging ache of your joints, and the faculties of sight, hearing and movement are severely limited, then a great deal of patience and maturity is needed to keep the enthusiasm and joy of youth, or even the childlike wonder of the imaginative faculties.

The fact is that coming to terms with, and accepting your mortality and eventual death is part of the maturing process, and some participation in the suffering of our common humanity comes the way of most of us. The Gospel does not promise us physical health and mental clarity to the end of our days, though good stewardship of physical and mental faculties does enable us to enjoy life to the utmost. Sickness and bereavement strike without warning, and it is well to prepare one's attitudes in the summertime of life for the inevitable disintegration of physical and mortal life, because then there can be a mysterious joy in embracing what comes. A sad picture is one of a man who has exhausted himself for money, success or prestige, for 'bigger and better' to whom financial and organisational growth is everything.

I hitched a lift some weeks back with a man who owns four businesses. His life was his work and he was proud to give himself unstintingly to it, and to incorporate his twenty-two year old son into the business concerns. Then his son had a fatal motor-car accident. The father told me that he had no place for religion, only for financial and business growth, and now the whole meaning of his life had been called into question. 'What is the use of work, of money, of success and ambition?' he asked. 'Now I have nothing to live for.' He asked me what I could make of that.

I told him that I would not presume to give him false comfort concerning his painful bereavement, but at least he had come to recognise the truth about the meaning of life. Life is only for love, and where love is lacking then nothing else has real meaning. He saw this but felt it was too late. He was a well-dressed, well-spoken man in his early fifties, and I wondered how long it would have taken him otherwise to realise the vanity of financial and industrial growth without a centre. Perhaps he would have found that centre increasingly in his love for his son, and this may have led him to see that the relationship of love is at the heart of all things. But now perhaps he will come to this more painfully, with much struggle and conflict, through suffering and bereavement. One of the heartening things that emerged as we talked was that he had a patient and loving wife, who had found, as he admitted, some consolation and strength in her religious faith. This couple were ushered into a profound awareness of the autumn of their own lives by a confrontation with the death of their twenty-two year old son.

I have a priest friend who once had to preach at a civic service in one of our northern cities. It was attended by mayor and aldermen, complete with chains of office and ermine-trimmed robes. He stood before them and said: 'Naked . . . you are all naked in the sight and presence of God. And one day we shall stand before him in our nakedness, with no chains of office, no ermine robes or covering for our sins and need. I want you to go home today, to lie upon the floor of your bedroom, cross your hands over your chest, and say: "I am going to die . . ." ' I don't know what they made of it all, but it was a salutary reminder, and within the prophetic tradition to preach thus. The remembrance of death is salutary, and it is part of the autumn of our lives.

The Groaning of Finitude

But there is another side to all this. There is something beautiful in the dying of things. I am an October child, and I feel the beauty and power of Dylan Thomas's autumn poetry, for he, too, was born in October, and it is of my own town of which he writes in his *Poem in October*:

It was my thirtieth year to heaven
Woke to my hearing from harbour and neighbour wood

And the mussel pooled and the heron
Priested shore
The morning beckon
With water praying and call of seagull and rock
And the knock of sailing boats on the net-webbed wall
Myself to set foot
That second
In the still sleeping town and set forth

It is a poem of precise, spontaneous overflow of wonder and melancholy. Few people could read it well, and it is to be understood intuitively, savoured in the heart, with a piercing sadness for its beauty. The last stanza gathers the tears and joy of the intervening verses:

And then could I marvel my birthday
Away but the weather turned around. And the true
Joy of the long-dead child sang burning
In the sun
It was my thirtieth
Year to heaven stood there then in the summer noon
Though the town below lay leaved with October blood.
O may my heart's truth
Still be sung
On this high hill in a year's turning.

A perusal of this poem, together with the sad melancholy and holy expectation of St Paul's letter to the Romans, chapter eight (especially verses 18 – end), underline both the finitude of our mortality and the mystic joy of anticipation of cosmic redemption that has always haunted the human heart.

The dying of things in autumn does not indicate a linear ending, but a cyclic process of redemption and return. The dying of Jesus is the corn of wheat which is buried in the ground, awaiting the miracle of new life in the springtime of resurrection. The putting off of our mortal frame is not the cessation of hope and love and life. At the beginning of this book I went out into our vegetable garden and orchard, and wandered among the autumn fruitfulness, marvelling at the sweet taste of the tomatoes which we had grown from seed. All around our small monastery there are fields of waving corn on one side, and fields of potatoes on the other. My line of vision carried me down the golden field to the wooded area in the valley where Dick Brook runs into the Severn, and Astley Church tower rises above the trees. That is where Frances Ridley Havergal's father, its priest, lies buried, and where she wrote many of her hymns. Her biographer indicates that she probably had the Severn in mind when she wrote:

Like a river glorious
  Is God's perfect peace,
Over all victorious
  In its bright increase;
Perfect, yet it floweth
  Fuller every day;
Perfect, yet it groweth
  Deeper all the way.

Autumn: the Season of Contemplation

In the Hindu tradition, when a man has come through the successive stages of his life, experiencing the phases of human existence in terms of dependence, learning, working, marrying, begetting and seeing his family grow up, he then may hand over his household burdens and concerns to his son, and either alone or with his wife, enter into a more contemplative phase in which, having laid aside worldly anxieties, and detached from the world, prepare himself for his last and greatest journey. There is yet another phase which he may enter, and that is the actual leaving behind of his family, home, possessions and all that has surrounded him during his earthly pilgrimage, in order to enter into the nearer presence of God in the forest, and thereafter in death.

There is a beautiful passage in Herman Hesse's *Siddhartha*, which depicts Siddhartha pouring out his whole life's longings and hopes to his spiritual guide, Vasudeva, and of the intuitive and receptive stillness that met him in Vasudeva's attentiveness and compassion:

> He felt that this motionless listener was absorbing his confession as a tree absorbs the rain, that this motionless man was the river itself, that he was God Himself, that he was eternity itself. As Siddhartha stopped thinking about himself and his wound, this recognition of the change in Vasudeva possessed him, and the more he realized it, the less strange did he find it; the more did he realize that everything was natural and in order, that Vasudeva had long ago, almost always been like that, only he did not quite recognize it; indeed he himself was hardly different from him. He felt that he now regarded Vasudeva as the people regarded the gods and that this could not last. Inwardly, he began to take leave of Vasudeva . . .

Eventually Vasudeva took his hand. He did not speak, but radiating love and serenity he led Siddhartha to the river and into an interior vision of yearning, sadness, and reconciliation and ultimate perfection. The knowledge, serenity, salvation and peace communicated itself to Siddhartha, and at last Vasudeva touched his shoulder gently in his kind, protective way, and said:

> 'I have waited for this hour, my friend. Now it has arrived, let me go. I have been Vasudeva, the ferryman, for a long time. Now it is completed. Farewell hut, farewell river, farewell Siddhartha.'
>
> Siddhartha bowed low before the departing man.
>
> 'I knew it,' he said softly. 'Are you going into the woods?'

'Yes, I am going into the woods: I am going into the unity of all things,' said Vasudeva, radiant.

And so he went away. Siddhartha watched him. With great joy and gravity he watched him, saw his steps full of peace, his face glowing, his form full of light.

Meditation

1 – 3 As in the *Meditation* for Spring
4 READ Romans 8:18-end slowly and reflectively
5 LISTEN to Vivaldi's 'Autumn' from *The Four Seasons*, or other suitable music
6 – 8 As in the *Meditation* section for Spring

Winter

The harvest is past, the summer is ended,
and we are not saved.
(Jeremiah 8:20)

The Winter of an Unfulfilled Life

Jeremiah has been called 'the weeping prophet', and the reason for that is that he could so truly identify himself with the pains, the sorrows, the sins and the blindness of his people, that the grief they should have felt, the sorrow they should have borne, the penitence they should have shown and the tears they should have shed, all became his. He realised the ultimate sadness of an unfulfilled life, an unfulfilled nation, an unfulfilled world. So his prophecy became weeping and his writings became lamentations. He was a man of sorrows, acquainted with grief, prefiguring the Suffering Servant figure of Isaiah 53, which found its ultimate fulfilment in Jesus, the Saviour of the World. Such is Jeremiah's indentification with redemptive pain and suffering that his words are put into the mouth of Jesus in our Holy Week reflections of the crucified Jesus:

> Is it nothing to you, all you who pass by?
>   Look and see
> if there is any sorrow like my sorrow.
> (Lam. 1:12)

The sadness of a life unfulfilled is not just that a man has frittered away his life, his seasons of opportunity, his springtime, summer and autumn of sowing and reaping in fruitfulness; nor yet that he faces judgment and privation for his neglect and sin; but rather that he does not fulfil that for which he was made. 'You have made us for yourself,' said St Augustine, 'and our heart is restless until it rests in you.' It grieves the heart of God when man spurns his overtures of love and mercy, and Christ weeps over Jerusalem not just because of its imminent judgement, but because he longed and yearned to gather the city to his heart of love, and Jerusalem resisted and turned away:

> O Jerusalem, Jerusalem, killing the prophets and stoning those who are sent to you! How often would I have gathered your

children together as a hen gathers her brood under her wings, and you would not.

I find it an impossible thing to understand – that a man can be faced with the divine Love and resist, reject, turn away. And yet such a tragedy seems terribly possible, and such a possibility and situation caused Jeremiah to weep, and caused Jesus to groan in Gethsemane and yield up his life upon the cross.

I remember a story I was told as a child, of a king who gave a staff to his jester, saying: 'If ever you find a greater fool than yourself, give this staff to him.' The years passed, and at last the old king called his jester to him and said: 'Jester, my friend, I am soon to embark upon a long journey.' 'Where are you going sir?' asked the jester. 'That I do not truly know,' replied the king. 'Well then, when will you return?' 'I shall never return,' said the king. 'What preparations have you made?' asked the jester again. 'Oh, I fear I have made no preparations at all,' came the answer. 'Sir,' said the jester, 'if you are taking a long journey to you know not where, and you will never return, and you have made no preparations for this last and important journey, you are a greater fool than I am. Take my staff.'

Of what use are crowns and thrones, money, success, reputation, ambition? The gaining of land, power, territory, the subjugating and ruling of nations – all these things are dust. But an unfulfilled life? The sadness of Jeremiah's cry is the sadness of seasons passed, of opportunities missed, of offers of love and mercy spurned, and of love unrequited. When the icy spell of winter covers the land, when warmth and light are but the memories of seasons gone, how then can hope be kindled, how then can life be sustained when no preparations have been made?

Winter and Contemplation

One of the loveliest winters I have spent was during 1983/4 in my mountainside hermitage in North Wales. The solitude began at the beginning of November and went on until May of the next year. I had no water inside the cottage, and one morning I woke to find that the peninsula was covered with snow. I went out with my water-bucket to the underground spring, but in the snow was unable to find either the path or the spring. It took me some time of digging and poking around before I found it, and I remember going back into the cottage and boiling some water to make hot coffee on that solitary winter's day. I was encapsulated, not only in a winter of solitude on a lonely mountain, but within the heart of God where I felt the warm heartbeat of his love and mystery.

It was during such a time that I came to a new understanding of my own finitude, mortality and death. I realised at a depth not experienced before that there was a sense in which to choose solitude was to choose death, in the sense that choice was no longer an option, and that life and death were no longer the issues that they had once seemed to be. I tried to communicate some of this in a chapter 'Deeper into God' in the book of that title, for when the Lord got me alone, free from all the busy distractions which surround me even in a monastery, I was forced to look into the abyss of my own bankruptcy, impotence and unspirituality, and realise again that the immensity of God's love and the depths of his grace are the only ground of my salvation.

I realised, too, that there was a wintertime of spirituality that I had to learn to encounter and embrace, it meant that there was a dimension in which I would lose my sense-feelings of God's loving presence. I would become devoid of all feelings of sweetness, embrace, joy and security and have no emotional or sensual props or supports. I would need to live in simple, naked faith in the darkness, in the cold, in the winter of the spirit. I had long said and believed that joy was not dependent upon feelings, happiness, mirth, glee or any natural or supernatural buoyancy. But to live in the contemplative winter of the spirit was another matter. It was no longer that I held on 'in spite of', but simply that I was held without thought, hope, volition or understanding on my part. It was as if I had to acknowledge that the cold, the darkness, the ice, the winter privation were simply *there*, and there was nothing to do but affirm it, recognise it and go on with basic, daily things.

I cannot properly explain or communicate all this, but just say that such a state exists, and in the midst of it you need not become anxious, terrified or even unduly concerned. For without feeling, you are held, and you know it to be so. All emotional and sensual 'highs' are over, but it is alright. Winter is the appropriate season to portray this situation, but the experience is not tied to a season. Such a winter can take place in the spring or summer – perhaps less in the autumn, but I'm uncertain about that. I am speaking, of course, of the mental and spiritual seasons of life.

The Winter of Death

And so comes the end. The time is when you no longer think that death is a 'some-day' possibility, nor that there are simply constant reminders of your mortality in the sickness and breavement all around you. Nor is it just that you have entered yourself into old age with the consequent loss of many friends. No, it is more than that. You are facing death in close proximity. It may be because of physical age – you have reached, or passed, your threescore years and ten. Or perhaps you have been diagnosed, at a much younger age, as suffering from a terminal disease from which there is no escape or evasion. At last it has come – the reality of death is *my* reality, and soon I shall be no more.

I can write about this only in three senses. First I have accompanied death many times in my medical and pastoral work. Second, I can (and do) often face it in imagination (lie upon the floor, cross my hands over my chest, and say 'I am going to die'). And third, I have faced it in the deepening of my contemplative life of prayer – especially in solitude. I have a long way to go at the time of writing, for I do not suffer any terminal illness, nor am I chronologically in close proximity to death. But I recognise in death not the enemy, but the friend. I realise that when St Francis welcomed 'Sister Death' he understood physical death not then as the wages of sin, nor as the extinction of being, but as the handmaid of the Lord who would lead him gently through the darkness of the tunnel, into the soft light of eternal love.

Death has to be faced, affirmed, accepted. It is a physical death, the 'emptying out of each constituent and natural force' as Gerontius experienced it – the laying aside of this mortal frame and its decay. Then there is a psychological process of dying and detachment from all worldly things, from all pride, ambition, possessions, relationships, so that the basis of your life is renewed in love. And there is a spiritual 'dying with Jesus', and indentification with Calvary-love that I am only just beginning to understand. St Paul experienced it in being crucified with Christ; St Francis knew it on the mountain of stigmata, and I must learn it gradually (please God) in the days, months or years that are left to me, if I am to fulfil the meaning of God for my earthly life.

Death and Rebirth

In the changing of the seasons and the cyclical movement of nature I see prefigured the dying and rising of Jesus. His transfigured, resurrected body was the same human body that had been laid in the tomb, but it was immortalised and glorified. What do I mean by that? I do not altogether know, save that the communication of 'spirit to spirit' that I already perceive, and the analogies which I see before me in the cycle of the seasons bear witness to a transmutation which I can affirm by faith. I am not as naive or as crude as to want to believe in the mere resuscitation of a corpse, but I do believe in the resurrection of the body – and I am not simply playing with words.

I believe that the early church was neither lying nor mythologising when its witness proclaimed the transfigured Jesus on the holy mountain and the resurrected Jesus after the cross. Of course such belief and proclamation is in line with the universal myth of the eternal return, the cyclic dying and rising God – but in Jesus I see him who is the fulfilment of all men's universal dreams, hopes and anticipations. If I am to die, I shall die in him; if I am to rise, I shall rise in him; if I am to live in glory, it will be the reflected glory of the only-begotten of the Father.

In some way all this will be lifted from the dimension of the individual to that of the corporately-personal, when the cosmic awareness of God's reality will interpenetrate all things and beings. There are no completely appropriate earthly analogies of time or space that can be applied. But the reality itself will both fill and surpass all my highest hopes, aspirations, expectations, analogies and dreams. Only one thing can I confidently affirm, and that is the eternal Love. And in that – in him – I shall rest.

Meditation

1 – 3 As in the *Meditation* for Spring
4 READ 1 Corinthians 15:1-28 slowly and reflectively
5 LISTEN to Vivaldi's 'Winter' from *The Four Seasons*, or other suitable music
6 – 8 As in the *Meditation* section for Spring

Conclusion: Lord of the Seasons

> 'Those that sow in tears shall reap with songs of joy; He who goes out weeping bearing the seed shall come again in gladness bringing his sheaves with him.'
>
> (Psalm 126:6f.)

Theology must be *believed* and *experienced* – and you can't have one without the other. Natural and revealed theology belong together – they are perfectly compatible and to separate them is heresy! The God who created the universe and who indwells every created thing is not a different God from the Father of our Lord Jesus Christ who reveals himself to us in the great prophetic tradition, culminating in the story of Jesus. The God of creation is the God of redemption, and every movement of the created order, the changing of the seasons, the variation of mood, the rhythm and pattern of the world, all these bear witness to the dynamic movement of God's providence and love.

If we are in touch with the deepest parts of ourselves, we must also be in touch with the seasons and the changing moods of creation. We realise that we experience the springtime of infancy and childhood, the summer of adolescence into adulthood, the autumn of middle age and maturity and the winter of old age. But in such a realisation, if we are open and flexible within ourselves, and pliable and resilient in the hands of God, we can capture springtime in winter, and feel within ourselves the recurring cycle not only of change and decay, but of hope and renewal.

It is never too late to tune into the harmony of the planets, the music of the sea and the melody of the seasons. The song of creation sounds throughout the cosmos, from the time 'when the morning stars sang together, and all the sons of God shouted for joy.' (Job 38:7) The rhythm of creation is the music of humanity, and if creation has been marred and spoiled, there are creative forces of renewal working towards healing and reconciliation, as there are in the experiences of human life. The eternal Word is the creative impulse and agent of God's healing in the world, and that same Word became incarnate in the person of Jesus of Nazareth. All the powers of God's Holy Spirit are at work in creation and in redemption, and behind it all is the mystery of God the Father, the fountain-head of the Holy Trinity.

If we can realise these things intellectually and experientially, in our minds and in our hearts, then we shall find that our very physicality will be renewed. We shall enter into the powers of the new creation and begin to participate in the eternal spring-tide which ushers in the dimension of eternity. For myself, I intuited these things from childhood, though I could not have communicated them then. And all through the seasons of my life I have been aware of the indwelling Spirit leading, guiding, teaching, providentially cleansing, forgiving and renewing me when I turned aside from the true way. And looking back upon springtime and early summer, I find myself now at that place where summer begins to give way to the echoing yearning of early autumn. In my psychological and spiritual experience I have glimpsed the icy cold of winter, and have known barren-ness, darkness and aridity. But never have I been forsaken in that wintry place, for I have been led there to experience for myself, and for others, the cold blasts of death and emptiness. But always, always there have arisen again the fragrant winds of love which gently blow over the garden of my heart, and the voice of my beloved who calls to me from the country of immortality and peace.

I am aware, as I come to the end of this book that we are all so different, and that the process of growth and maturity varies greatly in our experience of life. I am also aware that I am gradually moving from a powerfully evangelistic and busy communicative ministry to one which is increasingly hidden and contemplative. I can only guess and intuit where it will ultimately lead me – but certainly it will be into an ever-deepening experience of the love and mercy of God. What I have written here is wide enough and deep enough to encourage and enlighten your path. But reading a book will not necessarily set your feet upon the way, just as reading a map will not plant your feet upon the journey, or book-instructions on swimming or cycling will not immerse you in the water or give you balance upon the road. You must allow the truths in the book to become part of your living experience, open yourself to the creative Spirit of God, and allow the Lord of the seasons to widen and deepen your experience of nature and of grace.

Then as autumn changes into winter for you and for me, we shall experience again in our hearts the stirrings of the eternal springtime of love.

The Beloved

Blow gently over my garden,
  Wind of the Southern sea,
In the hour that my Love cometh
  And calleth me!
My Love shall entreat me sweetly,
  With voice like the wood-pigeon;
'I am here at the gate of thy garden,
  Here in the dawn.'

Then I shall rise up swiftly
  All in the rose and grey,
And open the gate to my Lover
  At dawning of day.
He hath crowns of pain on His forehead,
  And wounds in his hands and feet;
But here mid the dews of my garden
  His rest shall be sweet.

Then blow not out of your forests,
  Wind of the icy North;
But Wind of the South that is healing
  Rise and come forth!
And shed your musk and your honey,
  And spill your odours of spice,
For One who forsook for my garden
  His Paradise!

Katherine Hinkson